ARE YOU BRAND DEAD?

THE CREATIVEANS BRANDBUILDER™
APPROACH TO BUILDING YOUR BRAND

with illustrations, case studies, tips and exercises!

KIMMING YAP   YULIA SAKSEN   JUDY THAM

Published by Creativeans Pte Ltd.

Creativeans (Singapore), 512 Chai Chee Lane #03-03, Singapore 469028
Creativeans (Italy), Via Fratelli Roselli 5, Milan, Italy 20139
Creativeans (Indonesia), Level 23, Plaza Marein, Jalan Jendral Sudirman, Kav. 76-78, Jakarta 12910, Indonesia.

Creativeans Pte Ltd, Registered Office:
512, Chai Chee Lane, #03-03, Singapore 469028.

10   9   8   7   6   5   4   3   2   1

Illustration by Cheyne Koh, Creativeans

Are You Brand Dead?
ISBN 978-981-11-2233-0

Set in Avenir with Calibri and Raleway

Designed by Yulia Saksen and Kimming Yap

*Dedicated to you,
the business maker.*

Contents

Chapter 1
INTRODUCTION

Mr Brain opened his eyes and stared into emptiness. He could not move. *I must have died,* he thought as he looked at his limp mass. He saw figures walking around him, going about their business. He called out to them for help, but they could not hear him. He mustered his strength and lifted his hands, waving frantically. Finally, a figure approached him. *Yes, someone noticed me at last!* He heaved a sigh of relief and waited to be rescued. The figure came closer, but alas, he walked right past him. Mr Brain was in disbelief! *Am I invisible? Have I faded away?*

Is this the end?

Before we even begin, here's a look at the current business climate:

- A business fails every 3 minutes
- 96% of all companies fail within 10 years
- 250,000 new products are launched globally every year
- Email marketing response rate is 0.12%[1]

Like Mr Brain, many companies have the smarts, knowledge and expertise in their respective fields, but fail in capturing the market and achieving long-term success.

ARE YOU BRAND DEAD?

In our years of building brands, we have met many forms of Mr Brain; companies and entrepreneurs that are really good at what they do but are, unfortunately, brand dead. We often hear them remark that branding *is* logo design, branding *is* a form of marketing, and even disastrously declare that "if you build it, they will come".

It is our turn to ask you:

- Do you know what a brand is?
- Do you know what your brand position is?
- Do you invest adequate resources into nurturing your brand?
- Do you care about your brand at all?

If you say no to any of the above, I'm afraid that the diagnosis does not look good at all.

You are probably brand dead.

---

[1] cmocouncil.org

Now, the good news. The prognosis may not be as grim as it sounds. Fortunately in the branding world, there is still a chance to revive your brand and give it a brand new life (pun intended). And if you are starting a new company, this is the chance to start it right.

WHY SHOULD YOU READ THIS BOOK?

In our experience working with companies of different sizes and industries, we have encountered many businesses with enormous potential. Unfortunately, not enough effort has been put in to make branding the core of their business, either due to misconceptions of what a brand is or ignorance altogether. We have also heard many who said that branding was for big companies and an expensive endeavour. They are partially right; it is expensive because the big boys need a proportionally bigger investment to generate the kind of brand equity required for them, but they do it because it creates value that is far greater than what they spent. But if you have a small company, you can still possess big brand ambition. It is ultimately about administering the right brand strategy and executing it in a way that fits your company. This is, in fact, the main reason we have decided to come together to write this brand book of ours. We love working with brands, and we believe by providing you with the knowledge and tools of brand building, we can help your business succeed.

YOU CAN BUILD A GREAT BRAND

With a fundamental understanding of what a brand is and building it in the right manner, the dead can, and does, come alive. Surgeons follow strict surgical procedures to ensure their patients have the highest probability of survival. Similarly for branding, there is a methodical and correct way to building it, and you, too, can build a great brand.

And let us emphasise, what makes some brands work while others do not – *apart from hiring great brand consultants* – is your commitment. And that commitment needs to come from all levels of the organisation – from the CEO, marketing director, customer service to your security guard. You need, as we like to say in the branding industry, *buy-ins*. Everyone needs to believe in the brand and behave consistently with what your brand represents. Everyone needs to be the brand, understanding its position, adopting its personality and delivering what it promises.

BRANDING IS NO LONGER A CHOICE

If you still have doubts about whether branding is worth the effort, let's take a look at some numbers:

- According to Forbes, 250,000 new products are launched globally every year; it is a crazy amount of competition you are up against in this globalised world.
- Consumers are exposed to as many as 5,000 advertisements per day, so much so that they simply do not pay attention to them anymore.
- According to The Economist, brands account for more than 30% of the stock market value of companies in the S&P 500 Index.
- 20% of your customers will deliver 80% of your revenues – that is the importance of positioning.
- According to a 2015 CareerArc Survey, 75% of job-seekers consider an employer brand before even applying for a job.

You can't afford to ignore branding because branding is *your business*. Brands sell. Period. And if you don't do it, others will, and they will surpass you in the crowded marketplace.

WHO SHOULD READ THIS BOOK?

This book is crucial if you face any of the following problems in your business:

- You are trying to identify the unique proposition of your products/ services
- You are trying to differentiate your company from your competitors
- You want to increase the awareness of your company
- You want to improve customer loyalty
- You are looking to find ways to penetrate into new markets
- You need to attract new customers
- You want to increase the perceived value of your products/services
- You want to improve your company morale

This book applies equally to both B2C (business-to-consumer) and B2B (business-to-business) companies. There is a misconception that branding is only good for B2C companies. B2B businesses need branding too. In B2B cases, their products and services are not as straightforward as B2C.

So long as you are dealing with humans (and all businesses do),
Branding is important.

WHAT DOES THIS BOOK CONTAIN?

This book is written in a practical, easy-to-understand manner with instructional information and helpful tips so that you can build your brand as quickly as possible. Throughout the book, there are self-assessments and exercises for you to reinforce your learning and apply to building your brand.

The chapters are written in a methodological manner, following the system in our brand building programmes we use to help our clients.

Throughout the book, we have also included case studies of companies that have become successful brands in the markets they serve. Through the interviews, they offer insights into how branding works for them.

Last but not least, follow the adventure of Mr Brain as he accompanies you throughout the book in his attempt to get out of his predicament!

"We are what we do."

- ERICH FROMM -

Chapter 2
SO, WHAT IS BRANDING?

Mr Brain stayed still, wondering how he ended up in such a state. Memories started to flood in. Years ago, he was the smart, go-to guy for solving problems. He was very confident of his capabilities and had no problems.

Until competitors arrived...

First thing first. Let's get the biggest misconception of branding out of the way: branding is not about logos, name cards, letterheads and websites. Yes, these are useful tools to help you communicate your brand. However, they are not the brand itself, but just what they are – logos, name cards, letterheads and websites.

To understand branding, we need to first understand human behaviour because your customers (we believe they are humans) are the ones who will ultimately perceive and judge your brand. You need to know exactly what they want so that you can influence their perception and judgement positively. What do they see? What do they buy? How can you reach out to them?

WHAT DO PEOPLE SEE

Have you ever wondered what people see?

With such abundance of choices and information in our society, an average person today receives far more information than he can possibly process. In order to make sense of the world they live in, people rely on impressions and simplification of ideas to digest information and make decisions most of the time.

Whether we like it or not, stereotyping still exists. If we see a man wearing an Armani suit and driving a BMW, we tend to think of him as a successful person. And if your Facebook has a picture of you showing off a Kate Spade bag, your friends know that you want to be seen as a stylish gal who likes to keep up with the fashion world.

In other words, customers make judgements on what they perceive and are concerned about what your brand means to them. Perception is reality.

WHAT DO PEOPLE BUY?

People Buy The Brand, Not Just The Product

People have the need to reduce their risk (and stress) when they make a purchase and they do so by looking for a brand they trust or are familiar with. It minimises the stressful process of searching and processing information to make a decision.

When a person buys something, he tends to choose a product that he knows or has some recognition. The recognition may be real or perceived. In other words, he may or may not have purchased the product before, but he could have seen it somewhere or recalled an ad that featured it.

It's akin to reaching out to a person you know in an unfamiliar environment. If you are invited to a party and the room is filled with unfamiliar faces, chances are, you will talk to the first person you know or recognise. You will probably feel more comfortable with the person than a complete stranger.

When you create a brand and communicate it successfully, the familiarity of the brand becomes real to the consumers. Even though they may not have actually purchased the product before, if they have to choose between a brand they have heard of and an unknown name, *the answer is obvious.*

People Buy Lifestyle, Not Just The Product

When a person buys a product or service, he or she is also buying the lifestyle that is associated with it.

It is not just your product or service that they care about, but how it can help them achieve the lifestyle or social status they seek. A brand can also help a person define who he is or whom he aspires to be. For example, Korean beauty and cosmetic brands such as innisfree and Etude House have made in-roads in many countries due to the K-pop phenomenon that is sweeping across the world. Many K-pop fans buy these products because they desire the lifestyle of Korean celebrities and aspire to be like them.

Similarly, people who purchase a Tesla are likely to be early adopters of trends and technology. They want to be seen as someone who is ahead of others and of course, can afford the premium price of an electric vehicle.

And if the experience of using the product works out well (i.e., achieving the desired lifestyle or social experience), they are likely to stick to the same brand, even when cheaper or better products come along. That's when you achieve brand loyalty.

BRANDING VS MARKETING

In a recent conversation with a director of a holding company, one of us was told, *"Our board has a hard time seeing the value of branding — they see marketing as a cost centre, not a driver of sales."*

Wait a minute.

How did we go from branding to marketing in one sentence just like that? Let us clear this common misconception.

Marketing, in its most simplistic form, is the act of promoting your products or services. Branding, on the other hand, is *everything you do* that reflects what you are. Your business is your brand. Marketing is the efforts and activities you do to communicate your brand.

Branding is strategic. Marketing is tactical.

Without it, your business is simply an empty vessel that carries some products and services that are no different from any others. It will have no soul, represent nothing, and mean nothing.

Simply put, a brand says:

"This is what I am and what I represent. If you like me or are like me, join me."

Rather than convincing people to "buy me", a brand gets your target customers to choose your product or service over others because they can connect with you, and see it as the right match to their problem or need. It is getting your customers to say, *"Okay, I get it. I get the idea of what you are, and I want to be associated with you."*

Branding pulls. Marketing pushes.

WHAT DOES A BRAND ENCOMPASS?

Now that we understand the psychology behind human behaviour, let's summarise "What exactly is branding?" and "What does it encompass?".

As mentioned, branding is establishing *"This is what I am and what I represent. If you like me or are like me, join me."* in the customers' mind. It is the way to differentiate your business from your competitors in order to attract and retain your customers.

A brand encompasses 3 main components: Brand Position, Brand Identity and Brand Touchpoints. Each of these components plays a significant role in building a brand, and we will elaborate them in greater detail in later chapters. But first, we shall explain what they mean in broad strokes.

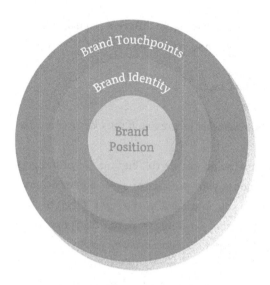

Brand Positioning is the "big idea" concept that guides your customers to perceive or experience your product or service in the way you want it. As mentioned above, people buy the lifestyle, not just the product, so Brand Positioning helps your customers see "beyond" your product, i.e., the aspiration and lifestyle they seek. **Brand Identity** helps you create the "image" that you want your customers to perceive, judge and experience. Finally, **Brand Touchpoints** are the channels or tools you use to communicate your brand to your potential customers and get them to be familiarised with it. This is where marketing plays a big role.

WHAT BRANDING IS NOT

It is imperative to know that branding is not the panacea that solves all business problems. Your business model, having a healthy cash flow, hiring the right people are equally important to keep your company afloat. However, putting branding at the core of your business will serve as the North Star that guides your business towards the success you envision.

Let's do a recap to see where your brand stands.

1. Explain in your own words what a brand is?

2. Explain in your own words what a brand is not?

3. What are the 3 main components of a brand?

-

-

-

Case Study:
The Sakae Brand

"Almost everyone in Singapore knows the Sakae brand. Even the taxi drivers who drop me off at our Sakae corporate headquarters have something to say about us," said Valerie Ong, the sales and marketing/corporate affairs manager of the renowned kaiten sushi chain restaurant.

Indeed, the reason so many people can identify with the brand is the very thing that made Sakae successful – their commitment to making high-end Japanese food accessible to most people. During the Asian financial crisis of 1997, Founder and Chairman, Mr Douglas Foo discovered a gap in the market – a demand for affordable Japanese food during a time where high quality Japanese cuisines, particularly sushi and sashimi, were relatively expensive with complicated pricing (prices were sometimes not even displayed on menus).

To make good and healthy Japanese food more widely available, Douglas studied the Japanese food and culture, and simplified the pricing of the dishes so that consumers were no longer afraid to try out such delicacies.

Mr Douglas Foo

Fast forward 19 years and today, Sakae Holdings has over 200 outlets worldwide and a portfolio of ten brands – Sakae Sushi, Sakae Teppanyaki, Sakae Delivery, Hei Sushi, Senjyu, Crepes & Cream, Sakae Express, Sachi, Kyo by Sakae and Nouvelle Events.

But interestingly, Sakae does not see itself as a food and beverage conglomerate, but an entity that is undertaking a global brand-building journey. Their ultimate goal? To have outlets at every corner of the world, with a Brand Name as synonymous with Japanese dining as McDonald's with burgers and KFC with chickens.

"Douglas likes to say that McDonald's has over 30,000 outlets, and we have 200, so we are only 29,800 away!" quipped Valerie as she explained the corporation's global ambition.

The enthusiasm in building a brand empire can be felt even amongst Sakae's employees, who are often brand ambassadors themselves. "As employees, we feel very strongly about the Sakae's brand and are honoured to be part of this brand-building journey. Maybe one day, when my grandchildren visit Africa and find a Sakae outlet there, I can proudly claim that I have contributed to the building of the brand," said Valerie.

It is not difficult to see the effort the company puts into branding. From the name, the frog mascot, its many merchandises, the consistency in design and colours to restaurant layout, you can easily spot a Sakae whether you are in Singapore, Malaysia or China.

But like other established brands, the challenge is keeping the brand contemporary and relevant in a crowded and fragmented marketplace so that they can continue to appeal to the fickle taste and preference of consumers.

"It's natural for older brands to constantly look for ways to communicate to their customers. Right now, we are putting more effort into boosting our presence in the digital space, particularly the various social media platforms. It's a process of marrying the past and the present, new ideas and traditional ways to attract the younger as well as the older patrons."

"Your brand is the single most important investment you can make in your business."

– STEVE FORBES –

Chapter 3
WHY BRANDING IS IMPORTANT

Mr Brain wondered what he could have done differently. *Did I miss something important? Something my competitors knew that I didn't?* He thought to himself. He searched his memory again, and suddenly, a word emerged from deep within, a word that had been mentioned many times to him but he had chosen to ignore because he was always too busy...

Brand.

We were often asked how important branding is. When we explained to the people who posed the question, a what-have-I-been-missing expression would inevitably register on their face. We would feel sympathetic because we knew how much opportunity their business had been missing out. There is an opportunity cost for not being a brand, and the longer you delay, the more you are losing out to your competitors.

There are so many reasons why branding is important, if not vital, to your company.

Let's go over the top 10 reasons for branding.

1. YOU WANT TO ATTRACT NEW CUSTOMERS

Customers have choices – the hundreds of products on the retail shelves that are competing for attention, or the many vendors vying for the same contract. Most people make purchasing decisions based on their first impression. You have that *one* chance to attract customers to buy from you rather than your competitors, so you need to make the best of it.

First impression matters. In fact, it only takes a few seconds – seven seconds, according to researchers – for a person to decide whether your product "fits me or not", "is the right solution to my problem" or "is a good brand to try out".

A strong brand makes a good first impression. Period.

2. YOU WANT TO BUILD TRUST WITH YOUR CUSTOMERS

Trust is the foundation for any sustainable, long-term relationship. Unfortunately, consumers are mistrusting products these days, and you can't really blame them. With so many companies behaving unethically, prevalent poor quality, a lack of transparency, etc., it is no wonder that confidence level is at all time low.

However, by staying true to the essence of your brand and delivering it well, you can build trust and ultimately brand loyalty, with your customers.

How do you build trust? Whether in life, relationship or branding, you build trust by making honest and genuine proclamations and communicating them consistently. It helps customers understand what to expect from your brand. When you make your promises known, it means something to them. They know you have thought things through, that you are serious about providing a good product or service, and that you know what you are doing.

3. YOU WANT TO INCREASE AWARENESS OF YOUR COMPANY

People remember iconic brands. Many times, the experience that is associated with it lasts a lifetime, and the thing that sticks in your mind may be beyond the visuals. It can be any part of your five senses – sight, hearing, taste, smell and touch – or your emotion.

To prove it, let's do a simple experiment.

Close your eyes and think about the first brand that comes to your mind. What do you remember about the product? The colour? The logo? The tagline, maybe? A catchy jingle? Or maybe even the aroma of the product (food or perfume) that filled the room? When you had your first bite? When you recall how you felt the first time you saw the commercial? Your emotion (excitement, anticipation, happiness) when you bought the product or played with it?

Whether the product is still available in the market or is already discontinued, chances are, you'll never forget your favourite brand and the experience you had with it.

By building strong brands, you can increase the awareness of your company and ensure that the brand is going to be remembered for a long time.

This is also pertinent to today's business environment where everyone is claiming a stake in the online world. A strong brand allows you to get your visitors to keep coming back to your website.

4. YOU WANT TO INCREASE THE PERCEIVED VALUE OF YOUR PRODUCTS/SERVICES

We are no longer living in a time where customers only want to satisfy their basic, functional needs. You want to manage and preferably increase the perceived value of your products or services. For example, when a young woman walks into Starbucks and buys a cup of mocha, she is buying more than just a cup of coffee. She is buying the entire Starbucks experience – the atmospheric interior, friendly service and quality of the coffee beans, to name a few. She is also buying a sophisticated and urbane lifestyle and is willing to pay a premium price for it.

Thus, customers need to perceive your brand as something of value to them before they can be convinced to buy your product. Your job is to find out what these perceptions are, and then build a strong Brand Identity to connect with them.

TRY IT YOURSELF

What pops and what doesn't? To find out, we suggest that you do a little experiment on your own. Go to a supermarket, walk down the aisles and identify the brands that capture your attention most. As you do so, observe and think about the following:

- Why did it make a good first impression?
- If it was a brand that you knew, was it because of brand recognition?
- What emotional connection did you have with the brands?
- Did you think that the brands were trustworthy?
- What did you learn from these brands?

5. YOU WANT TO IDENTIFY YOUR COMPANY'S UNIQUE PROPOSITION

A company is an entity, and an entity needs a unique proposition to attract and retain both its internal audience (your employees, investors and partners) and external audience (customers obviously, but also the media and potential employees).

By creating a brand that is well defined and easy to articulate, and maintaining a consistent Brand Identity, you are essentially uncovering your company's unique proposition with a distinctive voice. This way, your internal and external audience do not get confused between you and your competitors.

6. YOU WANT TO IMPROVE CUSTOMER LOYALTY

It costs more to acquire a new customer than to retain one. A returning customer has already bought into your brand and established a relationship with it. On top of that, there's a chance that these loyal customers would refer your brand to their friends and family, and such word-of-mouth referrals are powerful and effective means of promoting your product or service.

The stronger your brand, the more likely your customers will continue their relationship with you as long as their brand experience remains positive. And as your customer loyalty increases, so will your word-of-mouth referrals.

7. YOU WANT TO PENETRATE INTO NEW MARKETS

As your business grows, you will want to explore new markets, and some of the most common channels include distributorship, licensing and franchising. Few channel partners will be willing to work with you if they have not heard of your brand before. Particularly for licensing and franchising, a strong brand is a prerequisite to being successful in any new market.

A strong brand is also helpful if you are introducing a completely new product line. By associating your new product with a known brand (e.g. Chrome made Chromebook, or Jamie Oliver launched his kitchenware series), your chance of success will increase multi-folds.

It is also advantageous when you move your business from brick-and-mortar to e-commerce or m-commerce. A strong brand lets your customer know who you are immediately.

8. YOU WANT TO DIFFERENTIATE FROM YOUR COMPETITORS

Think about it: who are you competing with these days? Are your competitors local companies (because your focus is on the local market)? If you think so, you need to get used to the idea that there is no such thing as a local market anymore. With the pervasive use of the internet, leading-edge technologies and ease of travelling, you're now competing on a global scale, whether you like it or not.

Now, if you apply positive thinking and see that the glass is half full instead of half empty, competing in the global economy is not a bad thing at all. Think of the 7.4 billion potential customers out there. That changes your game plan, doesn't it?

How do you stand out from the hundreds of thousands of companies and brands out there? You need to differentiate, you need to have a unique value proposition and you need to define your brand clearly.

9. YOU WANT YOUR BUSINESS TO STAY FOCUSED

According to psychologists Matthew A. Killingsworth and Daniel T. Gilbert of Harvard University[2], "a wandering mind is not a happy mind". If you are distracted and unfocused in your business strategy and execution, or try to do too many things at the same time, it may result in unhappy-looking profits, unhappy employees and unhappy customers. It also scatters your resources, costing you more time and money in the end.

With a clear brand strategy, you are essentially building a long-term plan that helps you stay focused. It guides you in your product development, product implementation and marketing efforts. Whenever you or your employees are in doubt, you can always refer to the brand.

10. YOU WANT TO IMPROVE YOUR COMPANY MORALE

If your company morale is dropping, a clear brand position will inspire your employees. It also provides clarity and a sense of direction for them because they know exactly how to act, how to communicate and how to achieve the organisation and the brand's goals. Everyone is on the same page as to what the strategy is and where the company is heading.

If you were an employee, which company would you like to work for? Apple? Google? Facebook?

Why?

The most successful companies have strong and positive work culture, distinctive values, and most importantly, a robust brand. People seek more than mere monetary reward for their work. They want to work in a company they can be proud of. Therefore, it comes as no surprise that successful brands around the world attract the best talents.

---

[2] Bradt, Steve. (2010, November 11). Wandering mind not a happy mind. Harvard Gazette. http://news.harvard.edu/gazette/story/2010/11/wandering-mind-not-a-happy-mind/

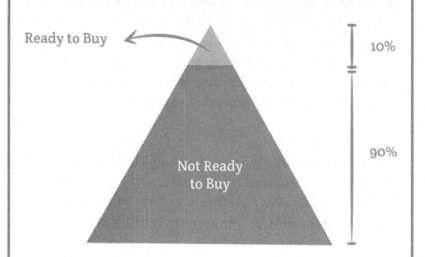

Ready to Buy

10%

Not Ready
to Buy

90%

ENGAGING THE 90%

In the diagram above, you can see that the top 10% of your potential customers are sales leads. They already have some knowledge of your product or service, and with some sales and marketing effort from your end, they will likely buy from you.

But the lower 90% are not, and that is where branding becomes a powerful tool because you start building relationship and engagement with the 90% very early on. And when they move up the pyramid, the first thing they remember is you![3]

---

[3] Holmes, Chet (2008). The Ultimate Sales Machine: Turbocharge Your Business with Relentless Focus on 12 Key Strategies. Portfolio.

Chapter 3 : **Self-assessment**

Every company has its own reasons to engage branding. Among the 10 reasons mentioned in the chapter, list the 3 most important reasons for you to brand your company. Include why you think they are your top reasons.

1st Reason
_____
_____
_____
_____
_____
_____

2nd Reason
_____
_____
_____
_____
_____
_____

3rd Reason
_____
_____
_____
_____
_____
_____

> "A goal without a plan is just a wish."

- ANTOINE DE SAINT-EXUPÉRY -

Chapter 4
5 STEPS TO BUILDING YOUR BRAND

What's the point of lying here and whining about the past? Mr Brain thought. Yes, I've made a mistake. Now I have to learn to fix it. It's time to pick myself up and move on. It's time to rebuild! He began to feel a glimpse of hope and excitement surging in him, giving him strength to sit himself up. But he remained invisible to others. *But, how?* He asked himself.

Where do I go from here?

By now, you should – no, you *have* to – believe in branding. And you probably should be asking how you can go about creating a great brand. Well, it's time to roll up your sleeves and start building!

FIVE STEPS TO BUILDING A GREAT BRAND

How do you build great brands? There is no magic or secret formula in building a brand. There is, however, a 5-step systematic approach that guides you through the process of brand building. We call it the Creativeans BrandBuilder™. This is a proven, tried-and-true process for developing a brand that we have successfully implemented with a large variety of clients spanning a range of industries.

What are the 5 crucial steps in the Creativeans BrandBuilder™? They are Brand Audit, Brand Positioning, Brand Identity, establishing Brand Touchpoints and Systemisation.

THE CREATIVEANS BRANDBUILDER™

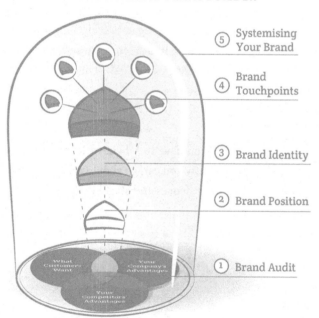

You will learn and put to practice each of the 5 steps in Chapters 5 to 9, and as you will see later on, every step is crucially interlinked and should not be skipped. Like a surgeon who operates on patients, there are protocols and procedures set in place to ensure the highest success rate of the surgery, *and you shouldn't in any case, trust a surgeon who doesn't follow protocols!* Similarly for branding, following a process will ensure that you achieve the brand that you envision, and that your brand will be effective and relevant.

STEP 1: BRAND AUDIT
Understand yourself, your customers and competitors to provide a clear direction for your Brand Positioning
To gain a deeper understanding of who you are and where you want to be, first, you need to conduct a thorough Brand Audit. A Brand Audit is a methodical assessment of your company's current position. Through the audit, you will uncover the strengths and weaknesses of your company, and identify the opportunities to improve and develop your brand.

A Brand Audit includes conducting internal reviews, gathering customer insights and analysing your competitors. Brand Audits can be conducted by brand consultants who have the acumen to conduct insightful interviews, focus groups and other research activities with your customers, employees and other stakeholders to get a true and unbiased picture of your current state.

STEP 2: BRAND POSITIONING
Formalise a brand position that will achieve your brand objectives
With the insights gathered from the Brand Audit, you are on your way to developing and defining the ideal brand position.

At the very core of branding is your brand position. It is the *"Who am I, really?"* statement that everyone, not just your CEO or marketing guys but everyone, in your company agrees with. The brand position is the very heart and soul of your brand, and should answer the question *"Why does your product exist?"*

Your brand position should be clear and easily understood by everyone (especially your customers). Here, the maxim "simple is beautiful" rules.

There is a method to identifying the ideal brand position, which we will cover in Chapter 6, that takes into consideration your customer base and market dynamics. Once you have clearly identified and agreed to your brand position, you can start to define the other important aspects of your brand, namely your brand essence, brand values, brand personality, and brand positioning statement. They will provide the "meat" to your brand "skeleton" and give it a stronger identity.

STEP 3: BRAND IDENTITY
Visualise and express your brand
Your Brand Identity defines how you want your brand to be perceived by your customers. It can be represented through visual elements, sound or other forms that entice the senses. Components such as graphic design, colours, and typefaces are tools often used to strengthen your Brand Identity. Applied consistently over time, these components will become essential features of your brand.

Here, you will create specific outputs that will connect your brand with your customers. Such Brand Identity tools include:

- Brand Name
- Logo Design
- Tone Of Voice
- Graphic Style

- Imagery Style
- Typography Style
- Colour Palette
- Brand Tagline
- Brand Identity Manual

STEP 4: BRAND TOUCHPOINTS
Develop an umbrella of touchpoints that communicate your brand cohesively and effectively

Brand Touchpoints are essentially contact points between your brand and the world. They can be physical (such as product packaging) or digital (such as a website), and they have a strong influence on how your brand is eventually perceived by your customers.

The key to creating cohesive Brand Touchpoints is consistency in your message and design. Be it websites, brochures, corporate stationery or other marketing collaterals, they have to be created with your Brand Positioning and Identity in mind.

STEP 5: SYSTEMISING YOUR BRAND
Achieve a shared vision for the long-term success of your brand

Branding is not a one-time endeavour. To be truly successful in your brand building, you need to integrate branding into your company and encourage your employees to embrace it as part of its culture. You also need to develop a set of systems, procedures and processes so that your brand becomes an organic part of your company.

Each of the above 5 steps will be extensively discussed in the following chapters. By following these steps properly, you will create a well-positioned, unique and consistent brand.

"*Branding is a key pillar amongst the other business functions in driving sales.*"

Mr Adrin Loi

Case Study: Ya Kun Kaya Toast

The success story of Ya Kun Kaya Toast is already widely known, particularly in Asia. Its rise from a humble coffee stall in Singapore in the 1940s to an international franchise chain today was nothing short of a miracle. Renowned for its toast, soft-boiled eggs and coffee, Ya Kun has successfully brought an iconic brand from the shores of Singapore to countries such as China, Indonesia, Japan, Myanmar, South Korea, Taiwan and Philippines.

We spoke with the executive chairman of Ya Kun Kaya Toast, Mr Adrin Loi about his take on the importance of branding for his company.

How important is branding to your company?

Branding is a key pillar amongst the other business functions in driving sales. Our past branding efforts, directly and indirectly, have raised the corporate profile of Ya Kun.

What do you think is the most important factor to consider when creating a great brand?

A great brand should accord exceptional and unique value to the customers. This value generally addresses a gap that the customers cannot and/or have not been able to fill amongst the existing brands.

What sets your brand apart from your competitors?

Our brand is backed by a track record of quality, value-for-money food and beverage, customer-centric services and a sense of inclusiveness with all our stakeholders. Our brand also embodies the hard work and sincerity of my father and the founder of the company, the late Mr Loi Ah Koon, and is elevated to the next level by the vision and acumen of the next generation of the Loi family.

Describe your company's Brand Positioning.

We strive to be the first point of recall when people think of authentic Singapore-styled beverage and toast and selected food that are uniquely local. We also endeavour to entrench in the minds of people that Ya Kun is accessible, affordable, amiable and appetising.

Describe your company's brand personality.

Ya Kun is synonymous with sincerity, heritage, reliability and attentiveness (service/customer-centric).

What are some of the creative activities your company has done to communicate your brand?

We have partnered special interest groups to enable its members to taste our food, for example, Dining in the Dark. We have also sponsored our beverage and toasts for selected events and occasions to educate the participants and attendees on what is truly authentic Singapore-styled food. We were also involved in fund-raising activities, such as Tsunami Relief and Local Foster Care Charity. On special occasions like Mother's Day, we offer promotional items in our menu.

> "Knowing yourself is the beginning of all wisdom."

- ARISTOTLE -

Chapter 5
BRAND AUDIT

Let's begin with me, Mr Brain decided. Have I been too busy to take a good look at my business? Have I been so blinded by my success that I ignored what my customers really wanted? Have I been so arrogant that I did not see my competitors coming?

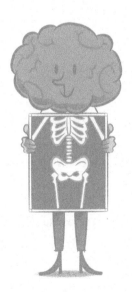

The first step to building your brand is to get to know yourself. Well. What are your strengths and weaknesses? What do your customers

think of you? What do your customers need? Who are you competing with? You achieve that by reviewing your company's vision, mission, values, products and strategies (or simply something that you lack), and your customers' current perception of your brand. You also conduct a detailed analysis of your competitors' strengths and weaknesses, current position in the market and so on. The entire process is called a Brand Audit.

THE CREATIVEANS BRANDBUILDER™

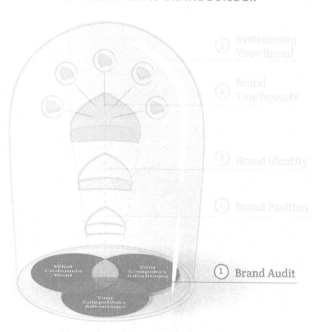

Companies frequently hire brand consultants to do the auditing work on their behalf. Getting a third party allows you an objective review and analysis of your current state.

However, do brace yourself for the truth, for the result may be shocking to some.

HOW TO CONDUCT A BRAND AUDIT

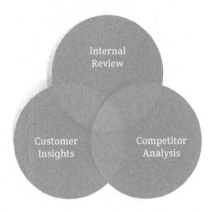

The objective of conducting a Brand Audit is to create your ideal brand position, which we will show you how in the next chapter. To conduct a Brand Audit, you will systematically go through and complete the 3 components of Internal Review, Customer Insights and Competitor Analysis.

COMPONENT ONE: INTERNAL REVIEW

First, a brand is built from within, and thus it is extremely important to know the current state of your business, for example, what are your business goals, and your strengths and weaknesses, because you will need real resources and commitment to build your brand. It is also equally important that you involve key stakeholders and employees in the internal review. A brand is built by people, and hence, everyone must be on the same page from the beginning. Like a ship chartering forward, it needs the full commitment from the captain to the crew to ensure it reaches the intended destination.

An internal review will ultimately ensure that you can deliver on your brand.

The review consists primarily of 3 areas – understanding your company, understanding your products/services, and understanding your sales and marketing strategies.

Now, ask and document the following questions:

Internal Review Questionnaire

AREA 1: UNDERSTANDING YOUR COMPANY

What is your company vision?

What is your company mission?

What are your company core values?

What are the important opportunities for your company in the future?

What are the threats?

What are your company's core competencies?

Who is your target audience?

AREA 2: UNDERSTANDING YOUR PRODUCTS/SERVICES

What are the strengths of your products/services?

What are the weaknesses of your products/services?

What makes your products/services truly unique?

How is your pricing compared to your competitors?

What new products/services are planned for the immediate future?

AREA 3: UNDERSTANDING YOUR SALES AND MARKETING STRATEGIES

How would you describe your company's sales and marketing approach?

What is currently your company's biggest sales or marketing problem?

What market segments do you sell to (by product category, demographic, geographic, etc.)?

What kinds of sales support or marketing materials are provided to the sales team or channel?

Answering the questions in these 3 areas will help you understand where you are and how to implement internal changes and improvements in order to move on to the next level. Spare no effort in listing out all the good, the bad, and the ugly. If your business is a service, collate the unique skill sets and expertise of your key employees, including yourself.

Also, your documentation should involve more than just words and reports; take photos of your company's premises, staff, products/ services, collaterals and also note down testimonials from employees. Doing so will help you visualise the state of your company, instead of relying on plain words.

COMPONENT TWO: CUSTOMER INSIGHTS

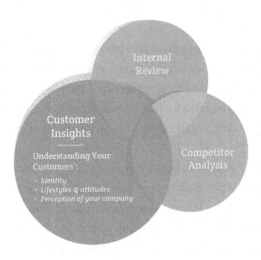

Defining Your Target Audience

Whenever we asked our clients who were their customers, many replied that they served all customers. You can't afford to sell to everyone. All brands need to give priority to their primary customers. Targeting a specific customer does not mean you are focusing on a tree and missing out the forest. It simply means focusing your energy and resources wisely on those who are most likely to buy what your business sells.

Here are 3 ways to identify your target audience:

1. Understand the problems that your products/services solve

The starting point in defining your target audience is to understand the problems that your products/services need to solve. Once you have a good idea of what these are, you can work out who is most likely to suffer from these problems.

2. Who will gain from the value in your offer?

Ask yourself: To whom would these problems be most troublesome? Who would have the most to lose by not dealing with these issues?

3. Look internally within your company

Another way of deciding on the right customers to pursue is to think about your company and its competencies. Do you have specific areas of expertise? Do you have unique knowledge of a specific geographical area? Are you better at getting on with certain types of people?

Sometimes, it is smarter to be different than to be the best or the biggest. It's hard to convince people that you are the best, but if you make yourself stand out in a homogeneous crowd, people can see your unique qualities more easily. It's called finding your niche. You may have a very specific market to serve, but if you serve them well, you have yourself a very strong position and a lucrative opportunity.

Now that you are clear about how to identify your target audience, here are the key questions you need to ask about your customers:

Customer Insights Questionnaire

AREA 1: WHO ARE YOUR CUSTOMERS?

Who is your target audience?

How do you want customers to perceive your company?

What factors influence them when purchasing your products/services?

What are the demographics of the users of the brand?

What are the demographics of the buyers of the brand?

AREA 2: UNDERSTANDING YOUR TARGET AUDIENCE'S LIFESTYLE AND ATTITUDE

What are the key values, attitude and lifestyle characteristics of the buyers of the brand?

What are the key values, attitude and lifestyle characteristics of the users of the brand?

AREA 3: UNDERSTANDING HOW YOUR CUSTOMERS PERCEIVE YOU

How do customers perceive your company?

What is the target audience's experience with and attitudes toward the products/services?

Does the company have a clear understanding of which brand benefits are most important to customers?

By now, you have a clearer idea of the characteristic of your customers. This component is very important to thoroughly examine and thought through. If you have difficulties learning about them, you should consider getting outside help to uncover the latent needs of your customers.

COMPONENT THREE: COMPETITOR ANALYSIS

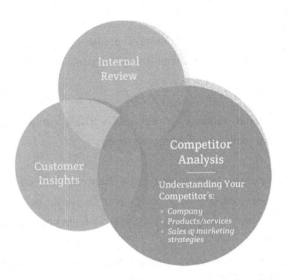

Written in the ancient Chinese book *The Art of War* by Sun Tze is this famous line: ***"If you know the enemy and know yourself, you will fight a hundred battles and win a hundred victories."***

Every business, no matter what product or service it sells, is bound to face competition. Even if you are introducing something completely new, you still have to compete with the "old way" of doing things or with whatever it is that people are currently spending their money on. Let's say you invent a radically new product (think iPhone back in 2007), your peers in the business world will eventually catch up with you sooner or later (Samsung, LG and Huawei).

To win your hundred victories, you need to know your competition. Before you say "C'mon, I know who my competitors are", stop and consider. Do you, really?

HOW TO DECIDE WHO ARE YOUR KEY COMPETITORS

To identify your key competitors, look for these usual signs:

They are always on your customers' shortlist – When your customers are considering who to buy from, these companies are always on their shortlist.

They offer similar products or services – These companies provide similar or even identical offerings as you do.

They are new entrants or substitutes – They may not offer the same products or services as yours, but deliver the same benefits to your customers and have taken market share away from your business.

To analyse your competitors, the followings are 3 areas you need to know thoroughly about them:

Competitor Analysis Questionnaire

AREA 1: UNDERSTANDING YOUR COMPETITORS

What is your competitors' vision?

What is your competitors' mission?

What are your competitors' core values?

What are your competitors' core competencies?

Who are their customers?

AREA 2: UNDERSTANDING YOUR COMPETITORS' PRODUCTS/SERVICES

What are the strengths of their products/services?

What are the weaknesses of their products/services?

What makes their products/services unique?

What are their pricing strategies?

Where are their products distributed to?

AREA 3: UNDERSTANDING YOUR COMPETITORS' SALES AND MARKETING STRATEGIES

What are your competitors' sales and marketing approach?

What market segments do your key competitors sell to (by product, demographic, geographic, etc.)?

What kinds of sales support or marketing materials do your key competitors use?

NOW YOU ARE READY TO POSITION YOUR BRAND

The exercises from the above three components will garner plenty of useful information that will help you proceed to the next crucial step. It's like going for a medical check-up to see if you have any health issues before you embark on an important journey in your life. If you have identified problems that need fixing, you should include ways to resolve the issues in your business plan.

It is time to whittle the information down to a Brand Position, which describes the core of your brand. In the next chapter, you will learn how to create it.

WAYS TO EXTRACT INFORMATION FROM YOUR CUSTOMERS AND COMPETITORS

There are several ways to uncover insights about your customers and competitors. You can use traditional methods such as interviews, surveys and focus group sessions.

In our work, we find conducting **Customer Journey** an effective way to learning more about customers and competitors.

A customer journey maps the emotional journey of a customer by representing the different touchpoints that characterise his interaction with your company and your competitors. Here is an example:

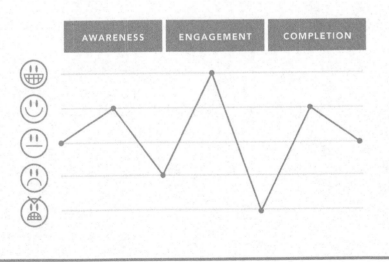

"*Products are made in the factory, but brands are created in the minds.*"

- WALTER LANDOR -

Chapter 6
BRAND POSITIONING

It is true, Mr Brain thought, feeling dejected. *I'd ignored so many red flags and missed so many opportunities. I thought my success would last forever... but it didn't. If I were to start again, what would I be really good at? How could I be better than others? Would that be what my customers really want? Wait... I think I know.*

Could I rebuild my business from here?

The key purpose of conducting a brand audit is to identify your brand position. Brand position is the place in the consumers' mind that you want your brand to own. It's the cornerstone for setting the brand attributes, values and identity you want your consumer to perceive when they think of your brand.

HOW TO POSITION YOUR BRAND

To position your brand, you need two things. Start with choosing the right space for your brand to own, and then define the space upon where you will build your brand.

Think of it as building your dream home. The first thing to do is look for the most suitable area to construct your dream home; a comfortable environment, nice neighbours, amenities, and so on. And you will also have some idea what the dream home would look like – colour, material, style, and the list goes on.

THE CREATIVEANS BRANDBUILDER™

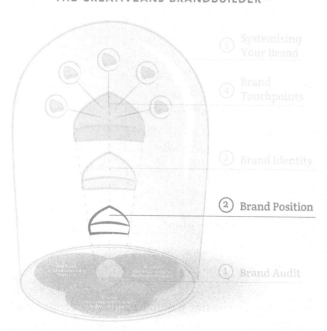

IDENTIFYING THE RIGHT SPACE FOR YOUR BRAND POSITION

After going through the brand audit, you should now have a clear understanding of your company, customers and competitors.

With all the answers you got from the brand audit, identify everything your target customers want – all the possible needs. Then map out all the benefits you can provide that others can't or where you can do better than anyone else – both functionally and emotionally.

Then list out what your competitors can provide that you can't or where they can do a better job than you – both functionally and emotionally.

From Customer Insights - What Do Your Target Customers Want?

1. _____
2. _____
3. _____
4. _____
5. _____

From Internal Review – What Are Your Company's Advantages?

1. _____
2. _____
3. _____
4. _____
5. _____

From Competitor Analysis – What Are Your Key Competitors' Advantages?

1. _____
2. _____
3. _____
4. _____
5. _____

So, where is the right space to position your brand?

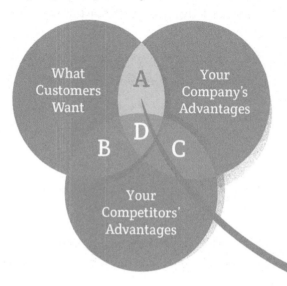

If you look at the diagram above, zoom in to **Zone A** – the intersecting zone where your advantages can best meet the needs of the customers while your competitors can't. This is the space where you can shine and outdo your competition. So focus all your energy to win in this zone and make it your brand's strategic position.

Zone B is the intersection where your competitors are better than you; forget about it because your competitor have built a strong bond with the customers here, so there is no place for you. There is where you will be fighting a losing battle. Also, stay away from **Zone C**. This is the space where both you and your competitiors do well but is outside of the needs of the customers. The customers do not care what is happening between you and your competitors; so shouldn't you. As for **Zone D** – the central point where you meet your competitors and customers – this is what we call a "war zone", the space where you need to be constantly fighting for business.

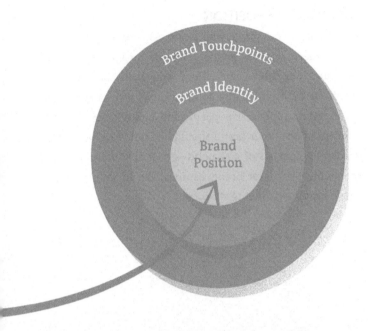

Brand Positioning At Zone A – What are your advantages that best meet the needs of the customers, and differentiate you from your key competitors?

- _____
- _____
- _____
- _____
- _____
- _____
- _____
- _____

DEFINING YOUR BRAND POSITION

You have now created the space where you should position your brand – the zone where you can uniquely provide for your customers' wants, where your competitors can't. Here, you shall start defining your brand position by building the foundation of your brand, and as the term foundation implies, it is permanent and will serve as the underlying concept of how your brand should be built. The foundation of the brand position consists of 4 structures that are interconnected and interdependent. They are: brand essence, brand values, brand personality and a brand positioning statement.

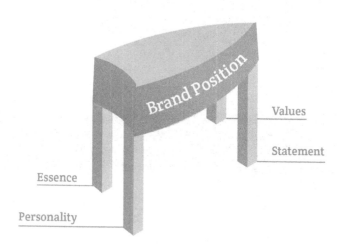

BRAND ESSENCE

Brand Essence is not a tagline. Your brand essence is the single intangible and emotional attribute that differentiates your brand from others and is true to the company. It is meant for internal use only. Crafted in a few words, it pinpoints the core of your brand and makes it visible for all stakeholders.

The best brand essence is:

Single-minded   You should be able to describe the essence in one to three words; anything more than three words indicates that the brand has no focus.

Emotional   It is based on how customers feel about your products/ services.

Unique   It is different from your competitors in the same category.

Experiential   It describes how customers experience the brand (example: driving a Volvo makes me feel my family is safe).

Authentic   The essence must be credible and your audience believes you can deliver on the promise.

Unchanging   It must be sustainable over time and doesn't change.

Meaningful   It should be important and can connect with your audience.

Scalable   It should allow brand extensions and continue to work as the brand grows.

Some brand essences of well known companies:

Disney	Fun family entertainment
Nike	Authentic athletic performance
Starbucks	Rewarding everyday moments

BRAND VALUES

Brand values explain how you deliver on your brand essence. They are keywords that define how you conduct your brand and describe your brand's approach, beliefs and what it stands for.

Brand values should be:

Authentic   They hold true to your company and reflect what you can deliver. You should not be distracted by industry standards or "best practices" of your competitors. Instead, focus on the elements that hold true to your company and can create real value for your audience.

Timeless   The values should be relevant and reliable regardless of the stage your business is in, and able to withstand changes in operating practices and cultural norms. Brand values should never change.

Unique   Brand values are like your brand's DNA – unique only to your brand. Outstanding companies often create values that truly differentiate themselves from others.

Examples of brand values of well known companies:

Coca Cola   Inspiring, passionate, fun
Toyota   Quality, value, reliability
Google   Imaginative, borderless, ease-at-use

BRAND PERSONALITY

Brand personality reflects the tone and manner in which you communicate your brand. It is the way a brand speaks and behaves. It means assigning human personality traits/characteristics to your brand so that it's behaviour is in tune with your brand essence and values. The brand personality also determines the way you carry out your brand identity and brand touchpoints.

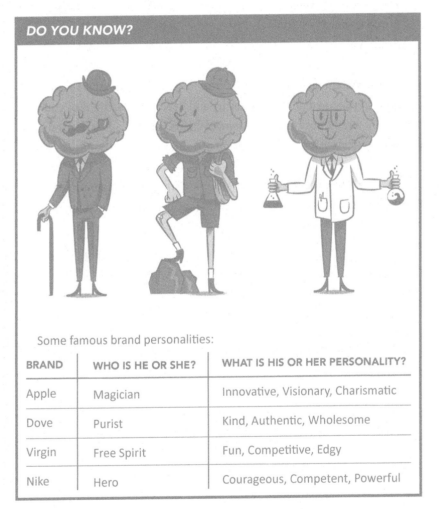

Some famous brand personalities:

BRAND	WHO IS HE OR SHE?	WHAT IS HIS OR HER PERSONALITY?
Apple	Magician	Innovative, Visionary, Charismatic
Dove	Purist	Kind, Authentic, Wholesome
Virgin	Free Spirit	Fun, Competitive, Edgy
Nike	Hero	Courageous, Competent, Powerful

BRAND POSITIONING STATEMENT

With your brand essence, brand values and brand personality, it is time to craft your brand positioning statement. It is the statement that sums up the position of your brand. Your brand positioning statement consists of the following elements:

- Target Audience
- Your Business Category
- Brand Essence
- Brand Values

Again, this statement is not to be confused with a tagline. It is meant for internal use to guide the marketing and operating decisions of your business. A brand positioning statement helps you make key decisions that affect your customers' perception of your brand.

Most people find writing a brand positioning statement a daunting task. Here's a simple way to get you started. First, use one of the templates below:

For ___ [insert Target Audience]___, the ___ [insert Company Name]___ is the ___ [insert Brand Essence]___ because ___ [insert Brand Values]___ in the ___ [insert Business Category]___.

or

For ___ [insert Target Audience]___, ___ [insert Company Name]___ is the ___ [insert Business Category]___ that delivers ___ [insert Brand Essence]___ because only ___ [insert Company Name]___ is ___ [insert Brand Values]___.

That should give you a basic statement to work with. Then re-write your brand positioning statement in the tone of your brand personality. If you're not a wordsmith, it is worthwhile to engage a copywriter to help you craft something that can well reflect your brand position.

AN EXAMPLE: CREATIVEANS' BRAND POSITIONING

creativeans®

Brand Essence: Crafting Brands

Brand Values: Creativity, Courage, Care, Comprehend, Conscience

Brand Personality: The Craftsman - Delicate, Thoughtful, Clever

Brand Positioning Statement: For small to mid-size businesses, Creativeans is the only creative company that crafts brands because only Creativeans has the courage to deliver comprehensive and creative solutions, with sincere care for our clients through deep comprehension of their needs and always working with a conscience for the good of our clients so they can transform into great brands.

DO ONE THING WELL

You don't need to have multiple or complicated "tricks" to create a strong brand position. You can do only one thing, but do it very, very well. For over 25 years, AirPlus International specialises in one thing: business travel payment and reporting, combined with superior data quality and high-touch local service. Coupled with their clear, consistent branding and strong emphasis on their brand values, they have maintained a strong reputation as the leading global business travel payment player in the industry for decades within their business category even with new competition, such as mobile payment, entering the market.

So think about it: what is that "one thing" for your brand? Find it, and follow through by making that "one thing" work for your brand.

Chapter Six : **Self-assessment**

What is your brand essence?

_____

What are your brand values?

_____

_____

_____

_____

What is your brand personality?

_____

_____

_____

_____

What is your brand positioning statement?

_____

_____

_____

_____

"A strong brand carries a company through good and bad times."

AirPlus
INTERNATIONAL

Mr Victor Cheng

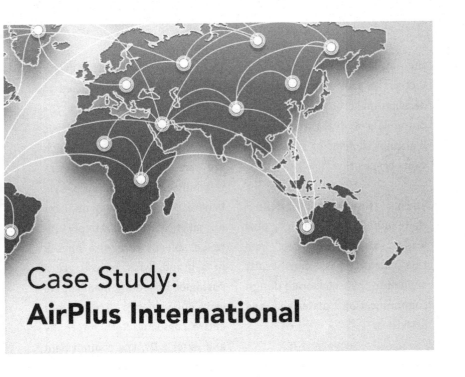

Case Study:
AirPlus International

Branding is not something reserved solely for B2C companies. B2B companies benefit as much, if not more from branding, especially in services where you need a differentiating factor to rise above the competition. Here is a case of how a B2B company uses branding to set itself apart from its competitors.

AirPlus International is one of the leading travel payment solution providers for corporations, serving over 46,500 corporations across more than 60 countries.

Established more than 25 years ago, it currently handles 154 million travel-related transactions per year. We spoke to Mr Victor Cheng, Head of Marketing APAC about the importance of branding for his company.

"In the payment industry, a strong brand carries a company through good and bad times. This is especially essential for a B2B company like us. Like consumers, professional buyers use the vendor's reputation as a shortcut that reduces risk and simplifies the evaluation process," said Victor. "In fact, B2B purchasing decision-makers consider the brand as a central rather than a marginal element of a supplier's value proposition."

AirPlus International defines their brand identity as a "global leader through expertise", and this identity is consistently applied to their corporate design, communication materials and activities.

As a specialised provider that serves a very niche market of business travel payment solutions, AirPlus International focuses on building brand recognition as well as offering a competitive advantage that gives customers access to unique transaction data not available elsewhere. Coupled with their brand promise of excellence, commitment, innovation and expertise, their customers know exactly what to expect from the company, thereby eliminating disappointment.

Having strong corporate values is also a way to stay committed to their brand and customers. "As a company, we place emphasis on our corporate values, which are personal ownership, respect, reliability and excellence. We believe branding is essential for all stakeholders. As it is important to be able to recognise oneself in a brand, whether you are a customer or a staff member, we want our values to permeate our entire company. Both internally and externally, the commitment towards these values is clear, and that makes it easier for the company to operate and communicate," explained Victor.

"AirPlus International focuses on building brand recognition as well as offering [customers] a competitive advantage."

"*Your brand is what other people say about you when you're not in the room.*"

- JEFF BEZOS -

Chapter 7
CREATING BRAND IDENTITY

Now that Mr Brain knew exactly where his faults and competitive edge were, he decided he would reinvent his business with a new identity – one that could truly connect with his customers and reflect who he is. He began to feel his strength returning to his feeble body. He was determined to try again, only this time, with a stronger conviction to do it right, to do it better than before.

Now that you have established a well-defined brand position, you are ready for step 3 – creating a brand identity and manifesting your brand in visible forms.

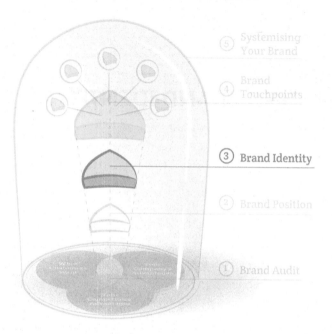

Firstly, what is a brand identity?

IT IS THE SKIN OF YOUR BRAND

You have completed the first step, brand audit and the second step, brand positioning. Those steps are meant for internal purposes and serve as a guiding compass. While brand positioning is the skeleton of your brand, brand identity is how you manifest your brand position on the exterior and make your brand visible for all to see and understand.

Your brand is ultimately how others perceive you. Hence, your brand identity must represent your brand position to ensure your brand is communicated in the way as intended and gets the attention it deserves.

WHAT FORMS A BRAND IDENTITY?

A brand identity is created by combining a set of brand elements in a consistent way to communicate what your brand stands for. The predominant types of brand elements are lingual and visual based, ranging from brand name, logo, graphic, tagline to colour, which is not surprising at all considering our ability to understand complex thoughts through words and images are basic human abilities. We will also examine other more sensorial types of brand elements that are increasingly used to differentiate brands in the already crowded marketplace.

SENDING THE RIGHT MESSAGE

A brand identity is also about sending the right message in the right context to the right audience. You may have the best of intentions, but if you commit the sin of sending a wrong or mixed message, it may cause confusion among your customers and end up losing them. If your brand is positioned to be high end, your customers should experience luxury. If your brand is positioned to be professional, it should paint you as an expert.

A classic example of sending the wrong message:

HALLMARKS OF A GREAT BRAND IDENTITY

A strong brand identity should fulfil the following 5 criteria:

It communicates your brand position

Your brand identity must first and foremost communicate your brand position. As the visible manifestation of your brand position, it must bring out the essence, values and personality of your brand so your target audience can feel, see and understand what and who you are.

It is uniquely identifiable

It can be distinguished from your competitors so your brand does not get lost amongst the thousands of other brand messages consumers receive every day. Remember, our brains are hard-wired to identify what's different, so it is okay to get creative with your brand identity.

It is simple to recognise

It is one thing to be creative, but another thing to be overly abstract. We are bombarded with brands every day, and this has overwhelmed and kind of numbed us. We do not have the time nor the attention span to pay attention anymore. Therefore, brands must be creative yet simple enough for your target audience to recognise it. Simplicity also creates stronger brand recall, so whenever your customers think of your product category, they will remember you first.

It is aesthetically-pleasing

A great brand identity is aesthetically-pleasing. By that, we don't just mean well-designed and beautiful to look at. The word 'aesthetics' comes from Greek, meaning 'having to do with the senses'. Thus, when we say a brand identity is aesthetically-pleasing, it must be able to touch our emotions and convey positive feelings about your brand. To achieve that means blending the right mix of brand identity elements that allow us to experience the brand in a multi-dimensional and multi-sensorial manner.

It can be easily reproduced

Lastly, it should be easily reproduced and applied to different types of media and channels. In this digital age, a brand identity's ability to flexibly transcend between the physical and digital media is more important than ever.

Now that you have understood what a brand identity is and what constitutes a great one, listed in the rest of this chapter are some essential brand identity elements.

BRAND NAME

When a child is born, the first thing that comes to the parents' mind is naming the child – giving an identity to the child to signify its arrival to this world. This symbolic gesture shows why naming a brand is so important. It is a coming into being; it means your brand has now taken shape and is real. Hence, for many, naming a brand is the first step. It is also why we put this as the first brand identity element. A brand name is the brand element that is least likely to change.

There are some things to consider when developing a brand name:

Distinctiveness Is it different from your competitors? Does it sound right in ordinary text and speech?

Meaningful Does it reflect the brand position, story and vision of your brand? A good brand name has to be something you believe in.

Appropriate Does it fit with the business and your brand position? Is it also culturally relevant?

Easy to spell and pronounce   Will most people be able to spell the name after hearing it spoken?

Protectability   Can it be trademarked? Is it available for web use? This relates to point one: the more distinctive your brand name is, the easier it is to trademark and find a web domain for it.

Types Of Brand Names

There are many ways to name a brand, and brand names can be broadly classified into 3 types:

Descriptive   A descriptive name indicates what the company, product or service is or does. Descriptive names are effective for describing the business nature, for example, Pizza Hut, Holiday Inn and China Mobile.

Acronym   An acronym is an abbreviation of a descriptive name, and can be quick to say and easy to remember, such as PETA, IBM and KFC.

Invented   Invented words are very powerful because they don't come with any baggage. They are empty vessels designed to represent a brand and can be compelling. Some examples include Twitter, Oreo and Adidas.

LOGO

You will most likely need the help of a designer to design a great logo, but your input and understanding of what constitutes a logo are essential because you want it to truly represent your brand identity.

First of all, what is a logo?

We are so familiar with logos that many people have the misconception that the logo is the brand. By now, you should know it is not. It is, however, still the most widely used and recognised element of a brand to symbolise one's organisation. From ancient coat of arm, marking livestock by branding them with a hot iron (that, by the way, was where the word "brand" came about) to present-day usage from corporations to institutions and music bands, logo is the most common way to distinguish your products or services from your competitors.

Types Of Logos

There are essentially 3 types of logos – logo symbol, logotype and combination mark. When deciding which type to use, consider how well it can communicate your brand to your target audience.

Logo symbol	Logo symbols are symbolic imageries that represent your brand. They can be literal or abstract and are great for conjuring the story of your brand (think Apple, Nike and Shell). When designing a symbol, it is good to leave some room for broader interpretation.
Logotype	A logotype, on the other hand, is your brand name stylised into a unique design to convey your brand message. Eligibility and ease of recognition are key considerations, and how well it can be translated into other languages if your business is international (think Dell, NASA and Disney).
Combination mark	A combination mark merges both symbol and stylised text into a logo to further enhance the clarity of your brand message. They can be designed to be used interdependently or separately. Think Starbucks (interdependently) and Toyota (separately).

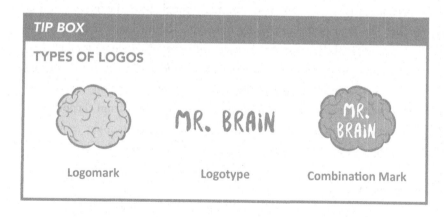

TIP BOX

TYPES OF LOGOS

Logomark   Logotype   Combination Mark

VISUAL STYLE

Visual style is a crucial form of brand identity that can quickly show the type of brand you are. Used correctly, it can be the glue that unifies the look, feel and tone of your brand.

There are 3 basic types of styles, namely the graphic style, imagery style and typography style. They are applied consistently to your brand touchpoints, and designers use them as style guides when designing for your brand.

Graphic Style - A set of reusable appearance attributes designed to visually translate the brand identity; for application across the various brand touchpoints to enhance brand recognition and awareness.

Imagery Style - A curation of imagery that helps communicate and differentiate your brand and engages the targeted consumers.

Typography Style - Typeface standards created to support the brand positioning, personality and information hierarchy.

THE POWER OF COLOURS

The most successful brands 'own' a colour (think IKEA, McDonald's and Starbucks). Our brain is programmed to respond quickly to colours and our memory of a brand colour remains longer in our mind than a name or logo. Colours influence how we feel about something, from the personality of a person to the taste of the food. It is also a key brand identity element used by brands to convey the right meaning and message to their audience.

Researchers found out that 90% of snap judgement on products are based on colours alone, and colours influence how consumers perceive the personality of a brand, which affects their purchasing behaviour. Hence, when choosing the right colour or colour palette for your brand, consider the appropriateness of the colour to your brand – does it 'fit' the brand?[4]

TIP BOX

COLOUR MATTERS

Colour is one of the most important choices you need to make when deciding on your brand identity. It has such a tremendous effect on people's psychology, mood and emotion that extra care should be taken when picking the right ones. Here, we've listed some psychological effects of common colours as a quick reference:

White   – Pure, innocent, clean and for some Asian cultures, mourning
Black   – Powerful, intelligent, slimming effect, sophisticated
Red   – Passionate, aggressive, lustful, and for some Asian cultures, auspicious
Orange – Happy, playful, warm, dynamic
Yellow – Cheerful, friendly, warm, warning
Green – Natural, cool, refreshing, tranquil, prosperous
Blue   – Calm, loyal, serenity, inviting
Purple – Royalty, mythical, magic

---

[4] Labrecque, L.I. & Milne, G.R. J. of the Acad. Mark. Sci. (2012) 40: 711. doi:10.1007/s11747-010-0245-y
Satyendra Singh, (2006) "Impact of color on marketing", Management Decision, Vol. 44 Iss: 6, pp.783- 789

A MEMORABLE TAGLINE

A good tagline will be remembered for a long time. Think of the number of times you have used "Just do it", or "Finger lickin' good" as a punch line.

While there are many approaches to creating a tagline, for example, functional, wit, wordplay and inspirational, do keep a few fundamental rules in mind:

1. It should communicate your brand position so that people know what you sell and what your brand represents.

2. It should be simple and short. Don't try too hard or say too much in a tagline because people won't take the time to decipher what you're trying to say.

3. It should be catchy and easy to remember. Preferably, a line that even children can repeat right away.

USE ALL THE 5 SENSES

As human beings, we naturally form a perception when we counter a new experience. Say someone puts a plate of kangaroo meat on your dining table. Your initial response might be to look at it (sight), hear what the waiter has to say about the dish (sound), smell it, touch it to feel the texture of the meat, and eventually, taste it. In other words, we often use all our senses to form our opinion about something we encounter for the first time.

The same applies to creating a holistic brand experience. We can engage more than one of the five senses of the customers to deliver a full sensory and emotional experience. Increasingly, successful brands are incorporating more than just lingual and visual elements in their branding strategies. Sensory branding is now a crucial component of a brand identity. People use all their senses in their daily experience, and by engaging these senses into their branding experience, you can evoke positive emotional as well as cognitive and behavioural responses.

You can engage the 5 senses in many ways:

Sight

This is the most obvious one, and is used by almost all brand experts. Visual tools such as colours, shapes, images, pictures, design, interior decor and lighting (for stores and restaurants) and even attractive models or staff (think Abercrombie & Fitch) are used to engage, stimulate and excite the visual sense.

Sound

The most common sounds used are commercial jingles (McDonald's 5-note "I'm lovin' it" tune) or the music played in stores or restaurants. Others include your brand ambassador's voice, slogan, ringtone or the little tune that plays when you turn on a computer (the Macintosh startup chime).

Smell

While this is not often used, it is gaining popularity among premises-based brands such as stores, shopping malls, hotels and even high-end hospitals. With scent diffusion systems that infuse scents directly into heating, ventilation and air-conditioning systems, brands use pleasant aromas to stimulate the olfactory system.

Such scent-induced branding often enhances brand recollection and improves the overall brand experience of the customers. Other tried and tested tools include placing fragrance ads (e.g. perfume) in glossy fashion magazines and displaying freshly baked cookies so that the mouth-watering aroma can permeate the mall (a.k.a Famous Amos).

Taste

While taste may be applied primarily to the food and beverage industry, non-edible brands are using it to enhance brand experience too. Popular cosmetic brand Lush, for example, has products that resemble delicious goodies, such as chocolate ice cream, to appeal to their customers.

Touch

Allowing your customers to touch and feel your products before buying them is also part of the brand experience. Zalora, one of the most popular online apparel stores in South Asia, has set up brick-and-mortar stores in addition to its online store so that their customers have a place to go to feel the texture of their apparels and try them on before making a purchase.

Here are 2 simple tests to check the effectiveness of your brand identity:

1. THE SWAP TEST

Swap part of your brand elements with that of a competitor or even a brand from another category. If the result is better or does not show any difference, your brand identity has room for improvement. A good brand identity is tailored for your brand and should only look good and right for it.

2. THE HAND TEST

Take any piece of your communication material and cover your logo with your hand. Can you still tell what brand it is? If it looks like it could come from another brand or is indistinguishable, then your brand identity is not strong enough. A strong brand identity must be able to express the brand without the brand name or logo.

*"A brand
is a living entity –
and it is enriched or
undermined
cumulatively over time,
the product of
a thousand
small gestures."*

Chapter 8
BRAND TOUCHPOINTS

Eager to show the world his new ideas, Mr Brain walked around the room and tried to talk to the people. But still, no one could see him or hear him. *I must look for the right ways to reach out to these people*, Mr Brain considered carefully. *I must think creatively to get them to notice me...*

You have now arrived at the 4th step of your brand building journey, where it is time for you to spread your love, and where your brand dances with your audience. Brand Touchpoints are the interactions your audience has with your brand. From a simple business card to a complex e-commerce website, they are the tools that carry and act as the ambassador of your brand.

In this chapter, we will discuss the different types of brand touchpoints, with a few examples for each of them. There isn't a concrete list of brand touchpoints, since they evolve over time with technology, trends and the way we communicate and conduct business. In fact, the more creative and innovative your brand touch point is, the better it is as it will set you apart from your competitors. A brand touch point is a means to an end; not an end in itself.

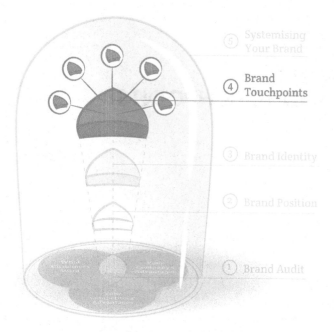

Types of Brand Touchpoints

Brand Touchpoints are points of contact with your external and internal stakeholders, from start to finish. There are external and internal Brand Touchpoints, and they exist in both physical and digital forms.

INTERNAL TOUCHPOINTS

Internal touchpoints communicate your brand internally. As mentioned in the beginning chapters, a brand starts from within, and it is imperative that the entire organisation is aligned with the brand. From your corporate stationery, work space to internal memo, these touchpoints ensure that your business walks the talk and is aligned with your brand, your people and your products/services.

Employees (we don't mean just your sales force) are your valuable walking advertisements if you do your branding right. By building a strong brand culture within the company, you can enlist all your employees to be your brand ambassadors. Wherever they go, they bring with them the brand identity and values to all external parties they meet in the course of their work.

Naturally, this requires a little overhaul on the mindset of the management as well as the employees. Getting your employees involved in idea-sharing sessions, seminars and other opportunities to voice their views would empower them with a sense of belonging to the brand. Also, remember not to leave the back-end operation staff behind. They are important touchpoints that are often neglected by organisations, and a weak link to the overall brand experience.

EXTERNAL TOUCHPOINTS

These are the touchpoints you use to communicate your brand to the outside world. This is where the sales and marketing tools and techniques kick in – from your product packaging, retail space, marketing collaterals to websites, they are your important brand ambassadors.

PHYSICAL AND DIGITAL TOUCHPOINTS

Physical Touchpoints are physical tools and interactions that communicate your brand for you to your target audience, such as name cards, corporate folders, brochures, packaging, T-shirts, key chains, coffee mugs and decals. Digital Touchpoints are digital forms of communicating your brand, such as websites, videos and social media. Both forms of branding are necessary, with digital branding gaining strong momentum in recent years as we live in an increasingly digitalised world.

In the rest of the chapter, we will share with you some specific ways to communicate your brand through both physical and digital brand touchpoints.

CORPORATE STATIONERY

Corporate stationery is the most visible aspect of branding. Often the first touch point (name card or email signature template) when you meet or communicate with someone new, these humble tools have a strong influence on the way your brand is perceived.

Again, consistency is the name of the game here, so get the following template designs done up:

- Business card
- Envelope
- Letterhead
- Email signature

PACKAGING

What is packaging? Packaging is a box, wrapper or container that holds or wraps the actual product. While that may be the functional definition of packaging, it is not its entire job. A good packaging does more than that. It is a vital component of branding, a marketing tool and a floor salesperson who screams "buy me!" – all combined into one. Your packaging has a strong influence on your brand, and ultimately, your bottom line.

A packaging is your last and best chance to make a sale.

A well-designed packaging fulfils the following:

- It is a physical manifestation of your brand. When consumers interact with the packaging, they should see your brand come alive.
- It communicates clearly the qualities of your product and allows for product lines or sub-brands to be developed in the future.
- It differentiates from the other products and has a strong shelf impact. Packaging is the only physical tool that fights directly with your competitors every single day – on the shelves.

ADVERTISEMENT

Advertisement includes both traditional and digital platforms, and the choice of media depends very much on your target audience.

Traditional advertisements such as TV and radio commercials, print ads in newspapers and magazines, billboards, and bus ads are conventional ways for brands to communicate to a wide audience. For small companies with a much smaller marketing budget or players in a niche market, it is still possible to be effective by using guerrilla marketing and online advertising, such as display advertising, and social network advertising.

EVENTS

If you want a more participatory form of touch point or to engage your potential customers on a one-on-one basis, event marketing is a good way to build relationships and garner direct response.

Some examples of event marketing include exhibitions, road shows, seminars, open houses and product launches. Because events allow your potential customers to participate and experience your brand, it can form a lasting and powerful impression.

MARKETING COLLATERAL

Marketing collaterals are effective and convenient tools to support the sales and marketing endeavours for your products or services. Here are our picks of the 6 most essential marketing collaterals you should have on hand:

- Corporate brochure
- Product or service fact sheets
- Corporate folder
- Product or service video
- PowerPoint presentation decks
- Press kit

WEBSITE

In the context of our globalised world, a website is the most effective tool to reach out to the international market. This is also most likely the first digital brand touch point your customers would encounter.

When creating a brand website, it is easy to overemphasise the features and functionalities and lose sight of its core purpose. A brand website communicates your brand and drives actions. To achieve that, your website should:

Allow a digital experience of your brand – your customers' digital brand experience is as crucial as the physical experience. Therefore, whatever branding strategy you have done should be applied here as well.

Communicate what your brand is – Focus as much on your brand identity as the features on your website.

Enable your customers to communicate with you – Your website is an excellent tool to exercise call-to-action (CTA). By allowing interaction between you and your customer, it helps form the beginning of a relationship.

So much has been written about how to create effective websites that I'm sure you know a thing or two about it. Thus, we'll reinforce the fundamental principle behind building websites: *It's not about you, it's all about your customers.*

In other words, your website should always cater to the needs of the users, and be:

- Easy to read (use fonts that are readable, keep your text short and simple)
- Easy to navigate (keep it simple, with intuitive layout)
- Easy on the eye (use colours that create balance and contrast to the text, and lots of white space)
- Mobile friendly (more users are searching for information with mobile devices)

BRAND VIDEO

A brand video communicates your brand position and identity in a narrative way. Usually 2 to 3 minutes long, the video can help to pull viewers to your brand as they immerse in your world through the sharing of the authentic side of your brand and featuring the real people and inner works. The video can also be shown (and made viral) beyond the traditional media such as TV commercials. It can be adapted for use on your website, mobile devices, social media and events. It is an effective communication tool for today's impatient consumers.

SOCIAL MEDIA

Increasingly, social media such as Facebook, Instagram, LinkedIn and Twitter are becoming essential touchpoints for brands. So, how can you make use of these platforms in branding?

As the word "social" suggests, social media is a space for digital social interaction between people; hard-selling is considered abominable here. Instead, you should use this space to connect with your customers. For example, on Nike's Facebook, you can hardly find any postings about sports shoes or apparels. Most of their postings are about aspirations of athletes or ordinary people, and this is what most companies do these days. This is the new normal.

There are so many reasons why you should place social media as a priority. Here are the top few:

- It provides instant, real-time connection with your customers.
- You can easily adapt your brand messages to reflect current trends.
- You can tailor or change content according to your target audience quickly.

TIP BOX

PITFALLS OF SOCIAL MEDIA

While social media has been lauded for its many advantages, it is also a double-edged sword that can potentially make or break your brand. Thus, beware of their pitfalls. The greatest nightmare for any business engaging in social media branding is a negative feedback gone viral. It has the potential to turn a simple misunderstanding into a PR disaster if it is not dealt with carefully.

Are you delivering your brand in unique ways? Compare your brand touch-points with your direct competitors. Focus on each of the touchpoints and identify how you can transform them into a unique and memorable aspect of your customer experience.

No.	Brand Touchpoints	My Brand	Competitor 1	Competitor 2	Competitor 3
1.	Corporate Stationery				
2.	Packaging				
3.	Advertisement				
4.	Events				
5.	Marketing Collateral				
6.	Website				
7.	Brand Video				
8.	Social Media				
9.					
10.					
11.					
12.					
13.					
14.					
15.					

"A strong brand is a critical component for the success of any business."

LHN GROUP
SPACE OPTIMISED

Case Study:
LHN Limited

LHN Group is not your conventional facilities management service provider. Focused on creating productive environments for small and medium enterprises and born-global companies, it takes old, unused and under-utilised properties and transforms them into creative, optimised space. With a robust portfolio of industrial, commercial and residential properties in Singapore, Indonesia and Myanmar, the company is taking the industry in Asia by storm.

Our chat with Mr Lorenzo Mariani, Creative Director of LHN Group, reveals interesting efforts made in their branding endeavour that helps them realise their business ambition.

How important is branding to your company?

In this ever-fickle consumerist society, a strong brand is a critical component for the success of any business. For a company like LHN, which is a holding of many different subsidiaries and companies in various sectors (real estate, logistics, car parking, security), branding will yield greater value if the company can leverage on the success of its business unit(s) to reap significant rewards for its other units. Hence, it has become paramount for us to strengthen our corporate identity via brand touchpoints such as stationery, website and online communication, printed collaterals and events.

What do you think is the most important factor to consider when creating a great brand?

Focus on your main objective. Also, paying attention to the details, even seemingly trivial ones such as the choice of paper for your name cards, tells a lot about your brand. An eye for detail is the key differentiator and makes a brand stand out from the rest.

In your opinion, what sets your brand apart from your competitors?

Our uniqueness lies in how our diversified portfolio of businesses is unified under the umbrella brand of LHN Group. We strive to build our brand equity through the creation of a productive environment that is driven by technology and optimisation of space, especially given Singapore's land scarcity.

We are embarking on different projects, from traditional domains such as commercial and industrial space to the logistics sector, and creating brands for lifestyle goods (Pickjunction), serviced office (GreenHub), self storage (Work+Store), and serviced residence (85 Soho in Myanmar). Our success hinges on our ability to do rigorous market research and ascertaining the UX/USP first, then focus on the design and brand management around the UX/USP.

Please describe your company's brand positioning.

We are a modern real estate provider catering to the different needs of contemporary entrepreneurs of all kinds - from SMEs to MNCs, freelancers to e-commerce resellers. LHN wants to be a leader in space optimisation, providing one-stop, value-for-money smart-space solutions.

Please describe your company's brand personality.

We are a trusted partner that supports the customers in identifying the right space based on their requirements. In short, trustworthy, dynamic, solid and objective-oriented.

What are some of the creative things your company has done to communicate your brand?

We have recently completed a corporate video. We are also in the midst of strategising a new way of leasing our space to keep up with new technology trends, as we believe that the crux is not what you communicate but how you communicate it. The medium is thus the key to a successful brand communication.

"A good system shortens the road to the goal."

- ORISON SWETT MARDEN -

Chapter 9
SYSTEMISING YOUR BRAND

As Mr Brain sincerely reached out to each and every one he approached, people started to notice. And they listened. *It worked!* He thought excitedly. *I am no longer invisible to them. They are actually listening and responding! This is fantastic!* But soon, he realised that there were so many people he needed to talk to, he simply couldn't do it alone. *I must work out a system and get others in to help me do this.*

And I have to make sure they don't make the same mistakes I did!

Congratulations! You have completed 4 stages of the Creativeans BrandBuilder™ – from brand audit, brand positioning, brand identity to brand touchpoints. You now have a brand! But that's not the end of your journey. As we said before, everyone in your organisation needs to get on board and stay committed for your brand to be successful in the long term.

This is what the last stage is about. You need to incorporate branding into your company's DNA and as an integrated culture. To make that happen, you need to systemise your brand so that it becomes an organic part of your organisation.

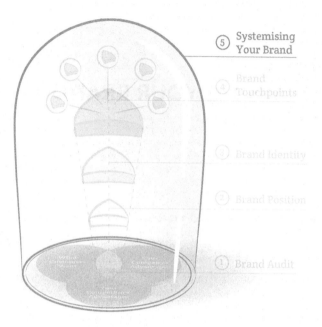

Systemising your brand is not unlike systemising your business. Essentially, you review the best way to implement the brand strategy and devise systems, procedures and processes whereby everybody within the organisation knows what to do and how to ensure consistency in your brand in the long run. If executed properly, a well-run system can make life easier for everyone, including your partners and suppliers.

CREATE A BRAND GUIDE

One of the most common practices is to codify your brand into a brand guide. The purpose of having a guidebook is to ensure that all the branding work you have produced so far is carefully documented. This way, anyone working on your brand in the future will have knowledge of your prior work and a specific set of instructions to follow.

The brand guide should include everything from your brand position to instructional details of your brand identity such as fonts, colours, logo, tone of voice and others. Apart from these essentials, you can also incorporate the brand systems and processes, such as the "who" (e.g. staff responsibilities in implementing and maintaining the brand), "what" (e.g. what to do with the logo, colours, etc.), "where " (e.g. the appropriate distribution channels or locations of your brand outlets) and "how" (e.g. how should employees deal with customers and business partners).

CREATE A DIGITAL REPOSITORY

You should store all your brand assets – stock photographs, images, logos (in digital form), profiles of key management staff, marketing collaterals, etc. in a digital repository where the right people can have access to. Also, have a proper system in place so that new materials are added only to this shared repository. This way, everyone is kept up-to-date with the latest stuff.

With a brand guide and a digital repository, your employees, PR agencies and creative partners will know what to do to maintain a consistent brand identity. It also provides clear, indisputable instructions to new staff, business alliances, licensees or franchisees about the use of your brand, thus ensuring that it will always have one look and one voice.

TRAIN YOUR EMPLOYEES

Next, train your employees to embody the brand. If your employees believe in your brand as much as you do, you'll have the most valuable and powerful communication tools in your hands.

To achieve this, your employees must buy-in the same vision, mission and values as you do (that's why we emphasise the importance of involving your employees when you conduct your brand audit in Chapter 5). When they do, they become your brand ambassadors.

But first, they must be empowered with the right tools and communication skills. And this is where training comes in. Do not assume that everyone knows or understands branding because not everyone has taken a class in branding.

Training comes in many forms. As brand consultants, we often deliver in-depth brand workshops for our clients' employees. These workshops help to define your brand clearly to your employees, drive home the message that they too can embody their company's brand and, at the same time, allow them to clarify any doubts or discuss any challenges they may face. This form of training can range from a half-day seminar to a comprehensive 3-day course.

Apart from formal training, department heads, managers and supervisors can also constantly remind their staff the importance of branding through on-the-job training. Even as simple a gesture as the boss showing up at his retail outlets and demonstrating the right way to serve customers is a good way to exemplify what it means to be a brand ambassador.

PUT YOUR BRAND SYSTEM INTO PRACTICE

Your employees can't perfect the art of branding if they don't practise it. When you think your employees are ready to be brand ambassadors, create opportunities for them to interact with external parties. These opportunities pertain not just to meeting existing or potential customers. Conferences, seminars, exhibitions, lunches and events of partners and customers are great chances for them to interact and network, especially for employees who are not frontline staff.

You can do even more, especially for frontline staff. We all know that frontline staff must be friendly, patient and knowledgeable in the products or services. But to go beyond the ordinary, you can train your customer service staff to interact well with others through your brand vocabulary.

Brand vocabulary is a list of common words and expressions that are suitable for your brand. If you don't have one, you can create a list and get your customer service staff to use them so that all your customers can enjoy a consistent brand experience. At the same time, your staff should also be aware of the negative words or phrases to avoid.

For example, if your customer service assistant did not know the answer to a question posed by a customer, instead of shrugging her shoulders and saying "Eh... I don't know", she could answer, "Please allow me to find out for you". The common phrase "that's okay" may sound right in a casual store, but not from the maitre-d' of a Michelin-starred restaurant.

Sometimes, saying the right words at the right time is all it takes to transform a customer's brand experience from an average to a superior one.

PUT TOGETHER A CHECK AND BALANCE SYSTEM

When your plan is working well, and everyone is starting to be comfortable, complacency tends to seep in, and that is the last thing you want.

We suggest that you put together a check and balance system to ensure that your brand objectives are met over the long term. One way to do so is to appoint a person or a team from within the organisation or externally as the custodian of your brand. The person or team, preferably an expert in the field and has been involved in the branding process right from the start, should be your point of contact for all matters concerning branding. The person or team should also be given the authority to make judgement calls when consulted by others.

Instead of appointing an employee to do the job, some companies retain external brand consultants to be their brand custodian. There are advantages to hiring external parties. First, as outsiders, they are objective and unbiased when offering advice. Second, as experts, they are capable of looking at the big picture and making decisions for long-term benefits. Brand consultants are also more in tune with the market trends, media and technology, which are all helpful to your brand.

PROTECT YOUR BRAND INTELLECTUAL PROPERTY

Last but not least, protect your brand! Your brand is the single most valuable asset and no one should take that away from you, so file intellectual property (IP) protections for your brand name, logo, slogan, designs, etc.

You can find out more about IP protection from your local Intellectual Property Office and The World Intellectual Property Organization (WIPO), the global forum for intellectual property services, policy, information and cooperation.

Here's a checklist of things you should do to systemise your brand. How many have you done?

No.	Brand Systemisation Tools
1.	Do you have a Brand Guide? ☐ Yes ☐ No If your answer is no, what can you do to implement one? _____ _____ _____
2.	Do you have a digital repository? ☐ Yes ☐ No If your answer is no, what can you do to implement one? _____ _____ _____
3.	Have you trained your employees to embody your brand? If your answer is no, when can you start? ☐ Yes ☐ No _____ _____ _____

4.	Do you have a list of brand vocabulary?	☐ Yes ☐ No
	If your answer is no, what can you do to implement one?	
	_____	
	_____	
	_____	
5.	Do you have a brand custodian?	☐ Yes ☐ No
	If your answer is no, who can you appoint?	
	_____	
	_____	
	_____	

Case Study:
Kingsmen

"Branding at its highest definition means a strategy that is very much built into the company's business strategy," said Mr Simon Ong, Co-founder & Deputy Chairman of Kingsmen Creatives Ltd. "Also, your brand is a living thing, and you need to constantly breathe new life into it to keep it relevant in the market."

"[The rebranding] built a robust fort for the company, helping them to withstand the waves of competition and the financial crisis that followed shortly after."

Simon does not simply spout branding philosophy; he actively applies it to his company. In fact, he has been a passionate advocate of branding, even at a time when the concept was new and largely unknown in Asia. As early as 1998, he decided that it was time to revamp his company's brand after more than 20 years in the design business. At that time, most people thought the idea of spending lots of money on branding insane, and it took him as long as 2 years to complete the brand strategy, with a significant proportion of the time devoted to convincing his company stakeholders that it was the right thing for the company.

"It is unnerving for people to venture out of their comfort zone because most of us are adverse to change. To get buy-ins from my directors, I had to gather everyone in Bangkok, lock ourselves up in a hotel and convince them that it was the only way to grow," he regaled.

Indeed, the move proved to be a winning strategy. Firstly, it helped them prepare for their public listing in Singapore in 2003. And in Simon's words, it built a robust fort for the company, helping them to withstand the waves of competition and the financial crisis that followed shortly after. Had they not strengthened their brand as a pillar that held their strategy together, the company might not have survived the Asian financial crisis in 1998 as well as they did.

The company's continual investment in branding has also earned them numerous awards and accolades. Kingsmen was the winner of the Most Distinctive Brand of the inaugural Singapore Promising Brand Award in 2002. Since then, the company has garnered at least one or more local and international design/branding awards every year.

Today, boasting a staff strength of 2,000 and 19 offices around the world, Kingsmen has persisted in keeping branding as an integral part of its DNA that holds the company together, directing staff to observe and share the same practices, views, goals and vision – from the core businesses to their own processes.

Kingsmen is now positioned as a leading communication design and production group in Asia Pacific and the Middle East with the ability to provide end-to-end integrated communication design solutions from exhibitions and events, retail and corporate interiors and thematic attractions and museums to brand activation. Their brand is also synonymous with design-led, quality and service-driven culture, and creative solutions.

Through their unofficial mascot Humpty Dumpty, which sits on a wall outside Kingsmen building, they communicate in a humorous way that their customers are always the "king" and they, the king's men who serve them in any way they can.

"Excellent firms don't believe in excellence - only in constant improvement and constant change."

- TOM PETERS -

Chapter 10
Nurturing Your Brand

Many years had passed since Mr Brain had his first close encounter with death. While he survived and thrived after a brief struggle, he would never forget the horrifying experience. He wanted to make sure that it would never happen to him again. It was too close a call, and he wasn't sure if he would survive another one. He took care, real care in making sure that he kept a close eye on his brand, and continued to nurture it over and over again...

In a study done by the American Enterprise Institute, which compared the Fortune 500 firms in 1955 with those in 2014, only 61 companies, or about 12% remained on the list. Almost 88% of the rest of the firms were dropped off. Some were bankrupted. Some merged with other companies. Others survive but have fallen from grace.[5] Some of the companies that reign for almost 60 years are Boeing, Campbell Soup, General Motors, Kellogg, Procter and Gamble, IBM and Whirlpool.

These companies come from very different industries and serve very different markets. So what do they have in common?

---

[5] Perry, Mark J. (2014) Fortune 500 firms in 1955 vs. 2014; 88% are gone, and we're all better off because of that dynamic 'creative destruction'. American Enterprise Institute

The constant turnover in the Fortune 500 reminds us that to survive in the market, companies have to continually innovate and re-invent themselves. The market is dynamic and ever-changing; so must your brand. Constantly re-looking and re-inventing your brand to serve the needs of the time is the only way for your brand to survive.

TAKING CARE OF YOUR BRAND

One of the common questions we get from our clients at the end of a branding exercise is, "Now that we have established a brand, we can just leave it as it is, right?" Well, think of your brand as your child. The new brand you have created is akin to your new baby, an entity that you have carefully conceived and given birth to.

In 10 year's time, this baby will turn into a child, a child with a different look, a different size and a different personality. Like your brand, the child will no longer be a fresh face to those who know him. Therefore, he will need to present himself and interact with his old and new friends (a.k.a your old and new customers) in a different way.

Add another 10 years and he will be a young man with, again, very different needs and traits. He will be matured by then, and able to do things he couldn't do in the past because of his accumulated experience and knowledge. His circle of friends (customers) will also change and most likely grow.

The same will happen to your brand. What will your brand be like in 10 or 20 years' time? Will you look at your brand the same way you do today? Will your customers look at your brand the same way in 20 years? We can say with confidence that the market will demand different ways to satisfy their needs and wants in a decade or two. Can you survive without changing?

TIME CHANGES, SO DOES YOUR BRAND

Companies like Boeing, IBM and Proctor and Gamble understand this very well, and that is why they re-invent themselves time and time again to keep up with the social, economic, technological and political trends.

This means that you have to monitor how your brand is doing in the market, and how it is being perceived by your customers. What is crucial to understand is that brand perception is owned by the customers, not by you. It is formed when the customers experience the brand, and therefore, is personal and subjective. That is why managing brand perception is one of the hardest things to do in today's landscape. With the additional pervasive use of social media, the power is now more and more in the hands of the consumers because they have the ability to share what they think of your brand instantly to everybody.

We agree that it is not an easy goal to accomplish alone. While we have given you the tools to build your brand, you can also consider getting professional help to maintain or bring it to the next level as your brand matures.

OUR PARTING WORDS

As brand consultants, if we could resuscitate the life of every dead brand we come across, we would happily do so. We hope that through this book, many self-helpers can breathe new life into their brands.

If you have made it to the end of this book, followed the steps faithfully, and successfully launched or re-launched a brand, you might have come to realise that the journey had been filled with excitement, wonders and surprises, along with challenges and frustrations. The exaltation from the experience will stay with you for a long time. I mean, you've just created something out of nothing and gave life to an entity that has never existed before. You're... a Brand Creator!

We also hope that you will continue to nurture this new life and empower it with possibilities and potential.

As long as you can imagine it, anything is possible.

ONE FINAL TIP!

We have other useful tools and supplementary materials available on this book's online portal to support you in your brand building journey.

Visit: www.areyoubranddead.com

ACKNOWLEDGEMENTS

Many friends, colleagues, clients and students have played an important role in making this book possible. We would like to thank all who have contributed ideas, provided us with advice and allowed us to test the book's material on their brands.

We are deeply indebted to the captains of industry who set aside the time to share their brand stories with us for the book's case studies: Mr Douglas Foo, Ms Valerie Ong, Mr Adrin Loi, Mr Victor Cheng, Mr Lorenzo Mariani, and Mr Simon Ong.

And a big thank you to all who helped make the interviews possible: Annie Ang, Amelie Marivain, and Charlene Sng.

We are particularly grateful to those who took the time to read the manuscript, gave us invaluable feedback and pointed out omissions and mistakes: Gyan Lee, Tan York Cheng and Giorgia Brusadin.

Special mention goes to the Creativeans team, especially Giorgia Brusadin, Cheyne Koh and Muhammad Zulfadli for their creative input, suggestions and patience for this 'side project'. And to Khairul Hussin and Sharina Khan for being the founding members of Creativeans so all these can happen.

To our families, we thank you for your support, love and for believing in what we do.

Lastly, we are thankful to everyone who has given us the much-needed encouragement to complete the book.

We are eternally grateful.

NOTES

INDEX

customers 22, 25, 28, 47-50, 60, 77

D

demographic 46, 54
demographics 49
designers 83
designing 82-83
differentiate 26, 61, 77
digital experience 96
digital repository 107
digital touchpoints 93

E

e-commerce 26, 91
email signature 94
exhibitions 95, 108
external touchpoints 93

F

focus group 55
focus groups 33

G

graphic design 34
graphic style 34, 83
guerrilla marketing 95

H

human behaviour 9

I

imagery style 83
intellectual property 110

K

keywords 64

L

letterhead 94
lifestyle 11-12, 49
lingual 77
logo 34, 77, 81-82, 107
logo design 34
Logomark 82
logos 81-82, 107
logo symbol 81
logo symbols 82
logotype 81-82

M

marketing collateral 99
marketing collaterals 35, 93, 96
marketing collaterals 107
marketing strategies 44, 51, 54

mission 42, 44, 52

N

name card 94
name cards 93

P

packaging 35, 93-95
perceived value 5, 24
perception 10, 85, 121
physical touchpoints 93
powerPoint 96
psychology 13, 84

R

relationship 22, 25, 28, 97
relationships 95
retail space 93

S

sales & marketing strategies 44, 51
sales and marketing strategies 54
sales and marketing tools 93
senses 23, 34, 78, 85-86
sensory branding 86
stakeholders 33, 43, 62, 92
systemisation 32

systemising 35, 105-106

T

tagline 35, 77, 85
typeface 83
typefaces 34
typography 35, 83

U

unique proposition 5, 25

V

video 96-97
visual elements 34
visual style 83
visual tools 86

W

weaknesses 33, 43, 45, 53
website 96-97
word-of-mouth 25

creativeans®

{pronounced Cre-a-ti-veans kriˈeɪti:/vi.ən/}

We are an interdisciplinary creative company with a strong pool of expertise and global presence. Guided by our approach and methodologies, we serve a single a mission: to help businesses craft brands.

www.creativeans.com

Our Approach

INTERDISCIPLINARY

We approach projects from the intersections of different disciplines and develop a solution for you that is unique and original. The result? Fresh perspectives and out-of-the-box ideas that solve complex problems through ways you'd never dream of!

FOSTERING CREATIVITY

We do not just provide design solutions; we foster true creativity in each and every piece of our work. We know what an outstanding design entails, and how to engage customers through creative means to enhance brand value.

HOLISTIC SOLUTION

We call it our lock, stock and barrel solution. One seamless solution for all stages of your business development, integrating branding, product design, packaging design and communication design. From idea, concept development, design, testing to implementation, each vision is carefully articulated into an unique, robust solution without losing its original intent.

THINK GLOBAL, ACT LOCAL

All the world's a stage. And on this global stage, we are the creators. Creativeans exist beyond the shores of Singapore. Our presence is also felt regionally and in Europe . We believe that being global allows cross-pollination of ideas, and the ability for us to look for solutions in a wider, international perspective.

BRANDING

As brand builders, we combine strategic and creative thinking to offer an integrated and holistic approach to increase brand value. We help conceive your brand positioning, express your brand identity and eventually, execute your brand touchpoints. In other words, the whole nine yards. We leave nothing to chance.

PRODUCT DESIGN

We transform your ideas and visions into profitable products that are customer-centric and design-driven. Through our team's industrial experience and insights, we uncover what is important to your consumers, and identify innovative ways to bring out the best in the whole product experience.

PACKAGING DESIGN

Our packaging design service helps you to advertise, entice and persuade. We design packaging structures and labels across multiple industries, such as fast-moving consumer goods, beauty, food and beverages, healthcare, and consumer electronics. We ensure high visibility and structural integrity of your packaging, and create experiences around your packaging so your products stand out on the retail shelf and become brands your customers will love.

COMMUNICATION DESIGN

Our communication design service aims at unifying and integrating our client's brand communications and marketing channels into one consistent and coherent message. Be it executing marketing campaigns, social media strategies or graphic design development across print and digital mediums, we make sure that the execution is done with strong impact and in accordance to our client's brand strategy rather than in isolation.

"Equipping organisations with the knowledge and tools to grow their in-house creative strength."

Creativeans Academy is our educational arm that designs and conducts programmes to equip organisations with the knowledge and tools to grow their in-house creative strength. From design methodologies to brand building, our programmes are conducted over three hours or full days, customisable according to the scope required.

WE WALK THE TALK

As practising consultants and creatives working across diverse industries, we know what we are doing and we bring the industry's best practises to you.

ACTIVE LEARNING

Our workshops are designed to be highly interactive and engaging. We believe you learn best when you are an active participant.

TAILORED THEMES

Our workshops are thematic and we fit every workshop to the nature of the organisation so you can apply what you learn immediately.

PROPRIETARY TOOLS

We unveil our methodologies and compile them into a tangible toolkit that you can take away to aid you throughout and after the workshop.

ABOUT THE AUTHORS

KIMMING YAP is a designer, brand consultant, educator and the managing director of Creativeans, an interdisciplinary creative company based in Singapore, Milan and Jakarta. Kimming is a leading expert on brand and design strategies, and has served clients in a broad range of industries, including lifestyle, fast moving consumer goods, healthcare, beauty, food & beverage, furniture, consumer electronics and government. He conducts lectures on the subject of branding and design regularly and sits on the judging panel for Singapore Prestige Brand Awards. He holds a Master Degree in Design.

YULIA SAKSEN is a designer, brand consultant and the director of Creativeans, an interdisciplinary creative company based in Singapore, Milan and Jakarta. As a consultant and strategist, she transforms clients' businesses into creative brands. She conducts lectures on creative thinking, and is a recipient of multiple design and business awards. She received her Master Degree in Design from the Domus Academy in Milan, Italy.

JUDY THAM is a writer, entrepreneur and adjunct lecturer. Her passion in writing has led her to establish One Elephant (www.one-elephant.com), a copywriting firm based in Singapore. She received her Bachelor in Business Administration from the National University of Singapore.

CPSIA information can be obtained
at www.ICGtesting.com
Printed in the USA
LVOW06s2341200917
549487LV00014B/634/P